★ ★ ★ ★ ★

WIT AND WISDOM OF

ROSS
PEROT

ISBN:0-929230-15-9

Contributing Editor: Sarah Dana-Hall
Cover Design: Carolyn Davis

Book Trade Ordering:
PUBLISHERS DISTRIBUTION SERVICE
121 East Front Street, #203
Traverse City, MI 49684
1-800-345-0096
or
Ingram Book Company
347 Reedwood Drive
Nashville, TN 37217-2919
1-615-793-5000

A NOTE FROM THE EDITOR

As I approached this project, I felt rather sure that in the best case scenario, when the task was completed I would be tired of the endless search through contemporary pieces for Ross Perot quotes. I figured the worst case scenario, I would be tired of Ross Perot. There was even a fear that as I researched deeper into the man's history, I would become disillusioned—that he wouldn't be who I was hoping he would be.

But as tired as I am at this writing, I actually appreciate him more than I did before this incredible marathon of microfiche and university libraries—mostly for his own tireless enthusiasm for one project after another.

And while there are those whose desperate job it is to find Perot's Achilles' heel before November, I can't imagine anything that could be 'exposed' that would dampen my appreciation of Perot's drive and ethics.

With my task completed, my scenarios are changed somewhat.

Now the best case scenario, I see, almost magically, Perot manages to use his love of the American people [notice I said people, not government] to create a new revolution in American politics. The worst case scenario [and saddest] is that Perot becomes a politician.

Sarah Dana-Hall, Contributing Editor

*Referring to Bush's re-election
campaign team—*

**"They're generally known as the
dirty-tricks crowd."**

U.S. News & World Report, July 6, 1992

"Take our country back."

Time Magazine, June 15, 1992

"For ten years [Bush's] fingerprints were all over creating Saddam Hussein and putting billions of taxpayer-guaranteed loans in Hussein's pocket."

Time Magazine, May 25, 1992

"I don't have to prove my manhood by sending anybody to war."

Newsweek, June 15, 1992

"There are individual years where I've paid well over $100 million in taxes. I just consider that a happy event, because if you're paying that much in taxes, things are going pretty well in your life."

Time Magazine, May 25, 1992

Perot seems to favor hard work and a—

"Simple answer."

Time Magazine, May 25, 1992

"I'm interested in what stories will come out next.

Tomorrow someone will have me meeting with extraterrestrials."

U.S. News & World Report, June 29, 1992

Admitting the 'Navy's unmeritocratic promotion system' didn't suit him, he said in 1971—

"The waiting in line concept was just sort of incompatible with my desire to be measured and judged by what I could produce."

Newsweek, June 15, 1992

✱ ✱ ✱ ✱

On wanting to know everything before coming to a conclusion—

"Did you see Saturday Night Live? On television once, I said, 'My style is I have to see it, feel and taste it.'

And Saturday Night Live added, 'And pass it through my lower intestine.'"

Time Magazine, May 25, 1992

✱ ✱ ✱ ✱

"... action, action, action ..."

Time Magazine, June 15, 1992

✷ ✷ ✷ ✷

His team could solve problems that have baffled other politicians —

"... without breaking a sweat."

Time Magazine, June 29, 1992

✷ ✷ ✷ ✷

"But the phone banks are going crazy with working folks saying, 'Why are you wasting your time on this? We're not [as] interested in your damn positions, Perot. We're interested in your principles.'"

Time Magazine, May 25, 1992

★ ★ ★ ★

Perot wants—

"... strong, growing companies that keep Americans at work."

Newsweek, June 15, 1992

★ ★ ★ ★

On why he thinks people want him to run—

"It has everything to do with people's concerns about where the country is and where the country is going.

There is a deep concern out there about the kind of country our children will live in that I don't

believe has surfaced in the polls yet."

Time Magazine, May 25, 1992

What he has to do to solve the problems—

"[It] won't be pretty."

Time Magazine, June 29, 1992

"... we've got to protect the job base."

Newsweek, June 15, 1992

On aggressive [rude] journalists—

"It's interesting that when people are rude or arrogant or condescending, the switchboard just goes nuts for three days, people signing up [to work on his campaign] because it makes them angry.

Time Magazine, May 25, 1992

"Putting more money into the government is a serious mistake."

And I have said we will not raise
taxes."

Time Magazine, June 29, 1992

"If I could wish for one thing for my
children, it's to leave the American
Dream intact, so they can dream
great dreams and have those dreams
come true."

Time Magazine, May 25, 1992

Perot likes to quote F.D.R.—

"Take a method and try it. If it fails,

admit it and try another; but above all try something."

Time Magazine, June 15, 1992

"People [should] go to Washington to serve, not to cash in."

Time Magazine, May 25, 1992

On May 29, 1992 Perot resigns from a club that excludes Jews explaining that—

"[It is] not the right thing to do."

Time Magazine, June 29, 1992

✫ ✫ ✫ ✫

Insisting that the trade with Japan would be revised to be more equal, Perot wants—

"... the same deal ... You are going to see the clock stop.

You could never unload the ships to this country, just never unload the ships."

Newsweek, June 15, 1992

✫ ✫ ✫ ✫

On campaign tactics—

"The process we have for selecting a President is irrelevant to getting a good President for the people."

Time Magazine, May 25, 1992

"[The formula at EDS was] a teaspoon of planning, and an ocean of execution."

Time Magazine, June 29, 1992

"We are now in deep economic voodoo."

Newsweek, June 15, 1992

★ ★ ★ ★

"The government should come from the people, and we should have a government that gives the people an effective voice.

The people feel very strongly now that they have no choice in their government."

Time Magazine, May 25, 1992

★ ★ ★ ★

"Texans looked smart in the past because GOD put so much oil and gas here."

U.S. News & World Report, June 1, 1992

After being honest about not knowing a thing about the Rio environmental summit, Perot says on June 11, 1992—

"Certainly I am an environmentalist, and any thinking, reasoning person is an environmentalist."

Time Magazine, June 29, 1992

"[The current tax code] is an old inner tube with a thousand patches."

Newsweek, June 15, 1992

"We have a political system that is driven by getting money."

Time Magazine, May 25, 1992

"... the Republican Party specifically has had a nasty campaign to redefine me in a negative way. 'Everybody has to be somewhere.' And I guess these guys need work doing dirty tricks."

U.S. News & World Report, June 29, 1992

"[Let's] clean out the barn."

Newsweek, June 15, 1992

"[Abortion] is a 'woman's choice.'

**... [however] it is absolutely irrespon-
sible for two thinking reasoning
human beings to get drunk, get high,
get pregnant and get an abortion just
because they act like rabbits."**

Time Magazine, June 29, 1992

**"Running up and down the halls of
Congress all day, everyday, are the**

organized special interests who have money that makes it possible to buy the television time to campaign to get re-elected next year.

There are no villains here. It's just something that has evolved."

Time Magazine, May 25, 1992

Despite Perot's obvious displeasure with the Bush White House he says about the President—

"Nice man, nice family."

Newsweek, June 15, 1992

Saying—

"I've never gone over a river half way,"

Perot says he is willing to spend $350 million on his campaign if needed.

It may be the first time donations have not been solicited from supporters for a candidate. At the time of the printing, despite running first in the polls, he has spent under $2 million.

U.S. News & World Report, June 15, 1992

A single-word comment on Quayle's criticism of Murphy Brown—

"Goofy."

Time Magazine, June 29, 1992

"Now make the Congress—make the White House—sensitive to the owners of the country again.

That's very important to me."

Time Magazine, May 25, 1992

"Leadership is this—

**... have a goal; have a vision; as-
semble a talented team; get it done,
go on to the next one."**

U.S. News & World Report, June 29, 1992

**"We cannot—it is morally wrong, this
is a fundamental principle—spend
our children's money."**

Time Magazine, May 25, 1992

How much will he spend on his cam-
paign?

"Whatever it takes to run a proper
campaign."

Time Magazine, May 25, 1992

"You've got to change the tax system
... it's got to be fair.

The current tax system is not."

Time Magazine, May 25, 1992

"I learned most of what I know from

my mother and father.

They never taught it—they just did it."

U.S. News & World Report, June 29, 1992

"[Bush] is whiny and hand wringing."

Newsweek, June 15, 1992

"What we have now is mud wrestling
and dirty tricks and Willie Horton,
and just stuff that everybody goes
into a feeding frenzy over.

It encourages virtually everybody

**who might be a good President not
to run."**

Time Magazine, May 25, 1992

*Perot has been criticized for hiring Ed
Rollins and Hamilton Jordan, although
he has stated—*

**"... there would not be a 'handler'
anywhere within a thousand miles of
me."**

Newsweek, June 15, 1992

His thought on government account-
ing—

**"The chief financial officer of a
publicly owned corporation would be
sent to prison if he kept books like
our government."**

Time Magazine, May 25, 1992

**"Only in America could you go in one
generation from a dad who hung his
ledger on a nail and never get to
finish high school because his father
died ... to a son who was able to
build a company that has computer
centers all over the world connected
by satellites."**

U.S. News & World Report, June 29, 1992

★ ★ ★ ★

"The grossest inequity I have seen in my adult life is when they created the new tax system and had the bubble where people like myself would pay at a lower rate than people who had a lower income."

Time Magazine, May 25, 1992

★ ★ ★ ★

His unpopular, however retrospectively insightful, view about the gulf war, which he strongly opposed—

"Only in America would you have a war, get it over with and have all the

heroes either be generals or politicians."

Time Magazine, May 25, 1992

✫ ✫ ✫ ✫

"Who created Noriega? George Bush."

Time Magazine, May 25, 1992

✫ ✫ ✫ ✫

"... for me to pay a lower [tax] rate than some guy making less than me is a joke."

Time Magazine, May 25, 1992

*Some lobbyists in Washington are
referred to by Perot as—*

**"These guys with their alligator
shoes."**

Time Magazine, May 25, 1992

**"It was obvious that my father loved
the people who worked for him, espe-
cially the blacks.**

**He would go see them every Sunday
after church and take me with him.
White people didn't go see black
people in those days, but he did."**

U.S. News & World Report, June 29, 1992

✫ ✫ ✫ ✫

"Who was in charge of antiter-
rorism? George Bush.

Who was in the middle of Iran-Con-
tra? George Bush.

Why didn't he just say, 'Well, I blew
that, right?'

As opposed to that everybody
shredded; everybody ran, ducked
and hid.

Everybody turned into Teflon, and
who got hurt?

The American people got hurt."

Time Magazine, May 25, 1992

✭ ✭ ✭ ✭

On an America of the people—

"With interactive television every other week, we could take one major issue, go to the American people, cover it in great detail, have them respond, and show by congressional district what the people want."

Time Magazine, May 25, 1992

✭ ✭ ✭ ✭

"... you will never hear the words come out of my mouth, 'we will do whatever it takes to win.'"

Time Magazine, May 25, 1992

On how to work with both parties—

"First, my Cabinet will be made up of a cross section of the best people in both parties ...

They'll be a cross section....

If you elected Solomon as President, the wisest man who ever lived, couldn't solve these problems....

Don't think I can alone."

Time Magazine, May 25, 1992

"[My dad] was my best friend—just the way that my son, Ross, is my best friend now."

U.S. News & World Report, June 29, 1992

"... unless you [the voter] stay in the ring with me after November, there's no point in doing this, because we'll be failures."

Time Magazine, May 25, 1992

On GM red tape—

"I could never understand why it

takes six years to build a car when it took only four years to win World War II."

Perot has been criticized for his dealings with GM. His frustration often showed.

Perot referred to GM board members as—

"Pet rocks."

Time Magazine, May 25, 1992

"If you look for me after the election, you won't find me doing what Presidents have been doing in recent years.

I will be buried night and day in meet-
ings with the leaders of Congress."

Time Magazine, May 25, 1992

"You don't take risks by leveraging
yourself.

That's what destroyed so many of
our companies in recent years."

U.S. News & World Report, June 29, 1992

"... if you ever see me get up in the
morning and throw rocks at Congress, just have me led away quietly,

because I understand that Congress is my equal."

Time Magazine, May 25, 1992

"I don't mean to compare myself to the Wright brothers, but they are role models of a sorts. If you read about them and study their work, you see they just had to fly.

They didn't believe those who said it couldn't be done. It was just inside them."

U.S. News & World Report, June 29, 1992

On working with Congress—

"I will be buried with leaders....

I will be listening, listening, listening to their ideas....

What will probably be some first-term Congress[person] who shouldn't have had an idea that good, but it's [the] best idea, and we take these ideas and we present them to the people.

The people say let's do it, and now we have a system out of gridlock and a system that works."

Time Magazine, May 25, 1992

Perot goes against the popular when he feels he is right, even suggesting that failing high school football players should be barred from extracurricular sports, Perot states—

"No pass, no play."

He is also for reducing class size to help students.

Time Magazine, May 25, 1992

"The thing I hate ... hate—not dislike, hate— is the strange life we have created for our President where he is totally out of touch with reality, and where he is fed and briefed, and I will not get in that trap.

I will break out of it."

Time Magazine, May 25, 1992

"The town hall is 20 times better than polls in terms of knowing what people think....

The town-hall reaction is after you're informed."

Time Magazine, May 25, 1992

"... there's a very clear record here that I get things done by building consensus, and that's what you have to do.

The point is, give the people a vote."

Time Magazine, May 25, 1992

"... eventually [my paper route]
wound up at the houses of prostitu-
tion, which my mother was not
happy about.

But the women there could not have
been nicer. They always paid me on
time."

U.S. News & World Report, June 29, 1992

"My life has not been limited to the business world.

For example, getting the North Viet-namese to change the treatment our P.O.W.s received was not a corporate event."

Time Magazine, May 25, 1992

★ ★ ★ ★

"... [Bush] was responsible for the savings and loans, and look at what it got us."

Time Magazine, May 25, 1992

"Again and again and again I've had to go build consensuses, get people to do things, and get them done, and I listen to people.

I don't order them around."

Time Magazine, May 25, 1992

"[Americans] realize they have been sound-bitten to death...."

Time Magazine, May 25, 1992

"You can't be a good, effective leader if you are isolated, and we have total-

ly isolated our President from reality."

Time Magazine, May 25, 1992

**"I can't tell you how many hundreds
of miles I rode [hitchhiking] in the
back of a pickup truck with a dog or
a pig or whatever for company.**

**That was a wonderful world to grow
up in.**

**You didn't fear anyone was out to
harm you, and people were mostly
very, very kind."**

U.S. News & World Report, June 29, 1992

"The point is, if the traffic is bad in New York City and I'm in New York City, I want to know that traffic is bad in New York City....

I will not shut down entire road systems so that I can drive from point A to point B without having to stop at a stoplight."

Time Magazine, May 25, 1992

"This is not about me."

U.S. News & World Report, May 11, 1992

"The greatest thing that would break my heart is if I got there and could not do the job for the American people, and that's the reason I've spent so much time [saying] that I can't do it by myself."

Time Magazine, May 25, 1992

In 1988, before the National Press Club, Perot criticized the Dukakis-Bush race as misleading Americans about the economy—

"They sounded like Lawrence Welk—'Wunnerful, wunnerful, wunnerful'—and we bought it."

U.S. News & World Report, May 11, 1992

✯ ✯ ✯ ✯

"[In the Navy] I had a very unfortunate experience with a senior officer who wanted me to give him the crew's recreation-fund money, for which I was responsible, to redo his cabin.

He also wanted me to give him liquor because I was the alcohol and narcotics officer.

I turned him down two for two."

U.S. News & World Report, June 29, 1992

✯ ✯ ✯ ✯

"I think people will be able to figure out who can get things done and

who has a record of not getting anything done and who has a record of
making promises and then not
delivering."

U.S. News & World Report, May 11, 1992

"Margot [is not] a Barbie doll."

Time Magazine, May 25, 1992

"[Americans] realize they have been
headlined to death...."

Time Magazine, May 25, 1992

✯ ✯ ✯ ✯

"Talk to any of the people who've worked with me, and they'll tell you that I thrive on controversy and debate.

I make decisions after a lot of discussion, and my goal is always consensus.... I see my mission as solving problems."

U.S. News & World Report, June 29, 1992

✯ ✯ ✯ ✯

"We run this country now by what the pollsters say. You know that and I know that, and you know down to your toes that both parties don't make a move until they take a poll.

If you ever see me doing that, just lead me away, because that is so goofy, you know.

It's not what's the right thing to do.

Let's take a poll and then follow the wind...." *NOT.*

Time Magazine, May 25, 1992

Regarding people he works with—

"If I treated people the way folks are claiming, they wouldn't stay with me for 10 minutes."

U.S. News & World Report, June 29, 1992

* * * *

Perot is quick to praise others when he feels it is due. In the past he has praised a variety of leaders including Jesse Jackson and regarding Mikhail Gorbachev he has said he is—

"... the most interesting leader alive.

The Washington Monthly, May 1992

* * * *

Concerned that upper management
was out of touch at GM, Perot paid for a
Cadillac survey—

"The results were fascinating.

Cadillac customers thought it was a
piece of junk.

Cadillac mechanics in the dealer-
ships thought it was a piece of junk.

Cadillac dealers thought it was a
piece of junk.

The guys working on the factory
floor said it was a piece of junk and it
was depressing for them to put it
together.

The engineers from Cadillac said it
was a piece of junk, but if we got
their bosses off their backs, they

could make it a world class car.

The guy running Cadillac says he's got some plans.

But the bosses at the top floors of GM thought it was the finest luxury car in the world."

U.S. News & World Report, June 29, 1992

"A lesson I've learned from the lives of great inventors ... the most successful people in the world aren't the brightest. They are the ones who persevere.

Thomas Edison is one of my heroes. He tried everything to make an

electric light until he finally hit it."

U.S. News & World Report, June 29, 1992

"I will ask for legislation to replace [government workers] who don't treat the owners of this country with a smile.

We'll get rid of arrogance—all this 'I've got a lifetime annuity here I can treat you like dirt' mentality."

U.S. News & World Report, June 29, 1992

"[Americans] want things fixed.

They want a guy to get under the hood of the car and fix the engine."

Time Magazine, May 25, 1992

"I'm not asking to be drafted....

I am not encouraging people to do this....

The push has to come from them."

The Washington Monthly, May 1992

"What you see is what you get."

Time Magazine, May 25, 1992

Perot's favorite adjective—

"World class,"

The Washington Monthly, May 1992

On the campaign to date—

"I find it fascinating. Irrelevant to choosing a president, but fascinating.

U.S. News & World Report, May 11, 1992

* * * *

On the notion that he won't have what it takes when the real campaign begins—

"We'll be ready."

U.S. News & World Report, May 11, 1992

* * * *

It's going to be an amazing election year.

Stay tuned!

INDEX